CLASSICO®
PASTA · SAUCE
ITALIAN
FOODS TO SAVOR

Welcome
to Classico's Italian Table

In celebration of *William Shakespeare's A Midsummer Night's Dream*, Classico® is pleased to present *Italian Foods to Savor*. Throughout these pages, you'll find more than 50 recipes that recall the graciousness and bounty of Italy's famed culinary traditions.

The opening scenes of the Fox Searchlight Pictures film adaptation of Shakespeare's romantic comedy reveal preparations for the Duke of Athens' Wedding Feast, with dozens of cooks, bakers and kitchen helpers lovingly laboring over heaps of the freshest, most sought-after meats, produce, pasta and seasonings in all the land. We at Classico® salute the passion, craftsmanship and reliance on the best ingredients available that have inspired Italy's renowned cuisine throughout the centuries.

More importantly, we take pride in the Old World craftsmanship that goes into our own passionately prepared sauces. Each of our 14 varieties is inspired by the authentic cooking styles and unique ingredients found in a specific region of Italy, from the pesto of Genoa in Liguria, to the fire-roasted tomatoes of Siena, to the sun-dried tomatoes of Capri and more. This means that with each jar of Classico®, you can easily bring to your own table made-from-scratch taste that recalls the heritage and tradition of Italian cuisine.

Start with our culinary tour of Italy on page 4 and find out more about the regions that inspire Classico's Pasta Sauces. Then, sample the recipes. You'll find a full-flavored Italian dish for every occasion, from café classics and hearty country-style fare for the family to Tuscan treasures to serve friends. And, for a memorable dinner party, you can entertain in grand style with the Wedding Feast.

Enjoy this celebration of the great foods of Italy, in all their regional variety. *Buon appetito!*

CLASSICO®
PASTA · SAUCE

ITALIAN
FOODS TO SAVOR

INTRODUCTION 4
*Discover the regional cooking styles of Italy that inspire the
made-from-scratch taste of Classico® Pasta Sauces.*

PIAZZA FARE 10
*Experience time-honored Italian favorites reminiscent of
Italy's cafés, pizzerias and humble trattorie.*

COUNTRY TRADITIONS 38
*Turn to this chapter for family-style recipes inspired by the
cherished recipes found in country homes throughout Italy.*

THE TUSCAN TABLE 66
*Delight in these simple yet artful specialties and see why Tuscan
cuisine is capturing the hearts of food-lovers everywhere.*

THE WEDDING FEAST 84
*Regale your friends with a sumptuous Italian dinner inspired
by "William Shakespeare's A Midsummer Night's Dream."*

INDEX 94

Produced by Meredith Integrated Marketing, 1716 Locust Street, Des Moines, IA 50309-3023.

Pictured on the cover: Spinach and Cheese Stuffed Shells (recipe, page 52)

Strolling through the open market
—William Shakespeare's *A Midsummer Night's Dream*

As you travel

from region to region in Italy, you'll soon find that there is no singular definition of Italian cuisine. Instead, each area boasts its own distinct traditions based on the unique, local ingredients that generations of families have grown, harvested and lovingly brought to the table. Come along as Classico® takes you on a tour of the treasured culinary styles that have inspired our uniquely regional sauces.

Preparing for the Wedding Feast
—*William Shakespeare's A Midsummer Night's Dream*

Mastery Made Easy

While there may not be one overall style of Italian cooking, cooks throughout Italy share a common culinary bond: their passion for making every meal a celebration of hospitality and tradition. This means made-from-scratch cooking is the norm, not the exception. Italian cooks will spend much of the day searching the markets for the freshest ingredients, snipping aromatic herbs from their gardens, kneading dough for homemade bread and masterfully preparing and simmering their flavorful sauces. Classico® infuses each jar of sauce with the same Old World mastery and unique, time-honored ingredients that Italian cooks have relied on for centuries. This allows today's busy American cooks to bring authentic, regionally inspired dishes to their tables without spending all day preparing a sauce. Travel with us from the north to the south of Italy, then cross the sea to Sicily, for an overview of the regional ingredients that bring made-from-scratch taste to every jar of Classico® Pasta Sauce.

Regional Inspiration in Every Jar

THE NORTH

Two Classico® pasta sauces are inspired by the region of Liguria, a thin crescent of land that is flanked by the Alps to the north and the sparkling Italian Riviera coastline to the south. Classico® di Liguria (Tomato Alfredo) Pasta Sauce is a creamy, luscious sauce that salutes the refined cooking style of the Ligurians. Herbs grow wildly and abundantly throughout the hillsides of Liguria, and they make their way into pesto, a classic sauce made of generous amounts of fragrant basil along with garlic, Parmesan cheese, olive oil and pine nuts. This much-loved sauce is a specialty of Genoa, and Classico® pays homage to this lively port city with Classico® di Genoa (Spicy Tomato and Pesto).

THE CENTER

Classico® di Parma (Four Cheese) Pasta Sauce was created in the spirit of the rich, sophisticated cuisine of the Emilia-Romagna region. This area is the celebrated birthplace of the delightfully sharp Parmesan cheese, which some claim has been made in the region for 2,000 years. In keeping with tradition, Classico® di Parma (Four Cheese) Pasta Sauce calls on world-famous Parmesan cheese as a flavorful and authentic ingredient.

Tuscany—that's Toscana to the Italians—offers a gentle, sun-blessed landscape of vineyards, ancient olive groves and stunning medieval cities of stone, often perched atop green hills. In fact, two of the most beautiful cities of Tuscany—Siena and Florence—and the uncomplicated pleasures of the table found in each, serve as the

In search of the freshest ingredients for preparing favorite Italian dishes
—*William Shakespeare's A Midsummer Night's Dream*

inspiration for two Classico® pasta sauces: Classico® di Siena (Fire-Roasted Tomato & Garlic) and Classico® di Firenze (Florentine Spinach & Cheese). The hallmark heartiness and simplicity of Tuscan cuisine also can be savored with Classico® di Toscana (Portobello Mushroom) Pasta Sauce and enjoyed with a glass of the region's Chianti wine.

Located in the center of the country, Lazio boasts the ancient city of Rome, once ruled by powerful emperors who conquered distant lands. These days, *la dolce vita*—"the sweet life"—reigns in this very cosmopolitan city.

The Classico® pasta sauces that celebrate this region would be right at home in the city's trattorie and cafés that come alive each night, serving up robust specialties that reflect the Roman love for life. Dishes are often prepared *all'arrabbiata,* or "in the angry way," with a smattering of hot red peppers. This is the same lively touch given to Classico® di Roma Arrabbiata (Spicy Red Pepper) Pasta Sauce.

Classico® d'Abruzzi (Italian Sausage & Fennel) Pasta Sauce celebrates the cooking styles of the hard-working people of the Abruzzi region. Here, people live simply in the remote and mostly mountainous terrain. The cuisine is rustic, and cooks enhance their specialties with spicy sausages, full-flavored cheeses, shaped pastas and fiery red chili peppers.

THE SOUTH

Campania is home to the beautiful Amalfi coast and sunny Naples, which has given the world many a culinary gift. The most famous of these is the humble pizza pie.

Enjoying the Wedding Feast in the formal garden
—*William Shakespeare's A Midsummer Night's Dream*

Throughout Campania, open-air markets brim with tomatoes, so it's no wonder the area is also credited for popularizing spaghetti with a vibrant red sauce. Classico® has recreated three delicious variations on the Neopolitan red sauce: Classico® di Capri (Sun-Dried Tomato), Classico® di Napoli (Tomato & Basil) and Classico® di Salerno (Roasted Peppers & Onion). And, Classico® di Sorrento (Roasted Garlic) Pasta Sauce, named for the city of Sorrento, adds a little southern-Italian spice to a traditional Roman dish.

THE ISLAND OF SICILY

The Mediterranean island of Sicily has been a crossroads of many a culture; hence, its cuisine has been influenced by the Greeks, the Spanish and the people of north Africa, among others. Sicily also boasts its own black-peppercorn-studded version of the sharply flavored pecorino cheese. Pecorino is at the very heart of Classico® di Palermo (Pecorino Romano & Herb), named for the coastal city of Palermo. The diverse and distinctive flavors of Sicily have inspired another Classico® pasta sauce creation: Classico® di Sicilia (Mushrooms & Ripe Olives).

Piazza Fare

Farmers selling their finest produce in the open market
—*William Shakespeare's A Midsummer Night's Dream*

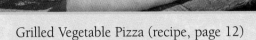

Grilled Vegetable Pizza (recipe, page 12)

Italian towns are famous for their piazze, or public squares. These piazze brim with lively cafés, pizzerias and family-run restaurants (called trattorie*) that serve up casual pizza, panini, soups and other much-loved classics like the ones you'll find here.*

Grilled
Vegetable Pizza

PIZZA CON VERDURE ALLA GRIGLIA

In Italy, you'll find a pizzeria near almost every city's piazza, as few foods are better suited to casual outdoor eating. Pictured on page 11.

1 (12-inch) prepared pizza crust
1 cup Classico® di Capri (Sun-Dried Tomato) Pasta Sauce
1½ cups (6 ounces) finely shredded mozzarella cheese
1½ cups chopped assorted grilled vegetables (see tip below)

1 ounce goat cheese *or* feta cheese, crumbled
1 tablespoon assorted chopped fresh herbs (such as parsley, basil, oregano and thyme)

Preheat oven to 400°. Top crust with sauce and mozzarella cheese. Place vegetables evenly over cheese layer. Sprinkle top with goat cheese or feta cheese and herbs. Bake for 20 to 25 minutes or until hot and bubbly. Let stand 10 minutes before serving.

Makes one 12-inch pizza (4 to 6 servings).

GRILLED VEGETABLES

Asparagus, eggplant, zucchini, bell peppers, red onions and mushrooms are great choices to use for the grilled vegetables in the recipe above. To prepare, precook asparagus pieces 3 to 4 minutes, and slice the other vegetables. Generously brush vegetables with olive oil. Grill directly over medium-hot coals until tender and slightly charred. Or, preheat oven to 400°; place vegetables in 13x9-inch baking pan and bake for 20 minutes or until tender.

Fire-Roasted
Tomato and Garlic Pizza

PIZZA CON POMODORI ARROSTITI E AGLIO

It seems there are as many versions of the pizza pie as there are pizzerias in Italy. Here's another creative rendition.

2 (12-inch) prepared pizza crusts
1 (26-ounce) jar Classico® di Siena
    (Fire-Roasted Tomato & Garlic)
    Pasta Sauce

Desired pizza toppings*
2 cups (8 ounces) shredded
    fontina cheese

Preheat oven to 450°. Place each crust on pizza pan if desired (pizza crusts may be placed directly on oven racks). Top each with pasta sauce, desired toppings and cheese.

Bake for 10 to 12 minutes or until hot and bubbly. Let stand for 5 minutes before serving.

Makes two 12-inch pizzas (8 to 12 servings).

*Top pizzas with your choice of sliced bell peppers (green, red and/or yellow), sliced ripe olives, sliced fresh or canned mushrooms, sliced pepperoni and/or chopped fresh basil or oregano leaves.

Chicken *Cacciatore*

Pollo alla Cacciatora

Cacciatore means "hunter," and according to one story, Chicken Cacciatore was devised by wives who prepared the chicken dish when their husbands came home from the hunt empty-handed.

8 ounces fettuccine, cooked as package directs and drained
2 tablespoons flour
1 teaspoon dried Italian seasoning
4 skinned, boneless chicken breast halves (about 1 pound), rinsed
2 tablespoons olive oil
2 cups (8 ounces) sliced fresh mushrooms

½ cup chopped onion
1 (26-ounce) jar Classico® di Sorrento (Roasted Garlic) Pasta Sauce
1 cup (4 ounces) shredded mozzarella *or* provolone cheese

In shallow dish, combine flour and Italian seasoning. Coat chicken with mixture. In large skillet, over medium-high heat, brown chicken in oil. Remove chicken from skillet.

Add mushrooms and onion to skillet; cook and stir until tender. Add pasta sauce and chicken. Cover; simmer 15 minutes or until chicken is fully cooked. Top chicken with cheese. Serve with *hot* fettuccine.

Makes 4 servings.

MUSHROOMS TO SAVOR

If you love earthy-flavored mushrooms, thank the ancient Romans, as they were the first to cultivate them. Today, favorite mushrooms in Italian cooking include the rare and much-sought-out white truffle *of Alba, Italy; the meaty and reddish-hued* porcino, *the earthy* cremino *and the fully mature form of the cremino called* portobello.

Chicken Cacciatore

Baked
Ravioli and Meatballs

RAVIOLI AL FORNO CON POLPETTINE

This hearty one-dish meal relies on flavorful convenience products—all you need to do is assemble, bake and serve.

2   (9-ounce) packages refrigerated cheese-filled ravioli *or* 1 (16-ounce) package
    frozen cheese-filled ravioli, cooked as package directs and drained
½   (20-ounce) package refrigerated *or* frozen cooked 1-inch meatballs (about
    20 meatballs), thawed
1   (26-ounce) jar Classico® di Roma Arrabbiata (Spicy Red Pepper) Pasta Sauce
1   cup (4 ounces) shredded mozzarella cheese
2   tablespoons chopped fresh Italian parsley (optional)

Preheat oven to 375°. Place ravioli in greased 11x7-inch baking dish; top with meatballs. Pour pasta sauce over meatballs; sprinkle with cheese.

Bake, uncovered, about 30 minutes or until heated through. Sprinkle with parsley if desired.

Makes 6 servings.

Baked Ravioli and Meatballs

Veal Cutlets

with Tomato and Basil Sauce

COTOLETTE DI VITELLO CON SALSA DI POMODORO E BASILICO

Veal cutlets are a favorite of Italian chefs throughout Italy because they cook so quickly.

8 ounces bow ties, cooked as package directs and drained
2 tablespoons flour
1 tablespoon freshly grated Parmesan cheese
Dash pepper
¾ pound veal cutlets, sliced ⅛ inch thick

2 tablespoons olive oil
1 (26-ounce) jar Classico® di Napoli (Tomato & Basil) Pasta Sauce
½ cup (2 ounces) shredded mozzarella cheese

In shallow dish, combine flour, Parmesan cheese and pepper. Dip meat into flour mixture, coating both sides well. In 12-inch skillet, over medium heat, cook meat in oil about 2 minutes or until light brown, turning once. Remove meat, reserving drippings in skillet. Set meat aside.

Add pasta sauce to skillet. Bring to a boil; reduce heat. Cover; simmer for 5 minutes.

Return meat to skillet; heat through. Serve over *hot* bow ties. Sprinkle with mozzarella cheese.

Makes 4 servings.

Pasta with Lamb Sauce

PASTA CON SUGO DI AGNELLO

Shepherding is a way of life for many people in the Abruzzi and Molise regions, inspiring this hearty lamb dish.

8 ounces fusilli, cooked as package
　directs and drained
1 pound ground lamb
½ cup dry white wine
1 (26-ounce) jar Classico® di Siena
　(Fire-Roasted Tomato & Garlic)
　Pasta Sauce

2 teaspoons chopped fresh savory
　or ¼ to ½ teaspoon dried
　savory leaves
½ teaspoon salt
¼ teaspoon pepper

In large saucepan, over medium heat, cook lamb until browned; pour off fat. Stir in white wine. Bring to a boil over high heat; continue boiling rapidly until most of the wine has evaporated, about 2 minutes, stirring occasionally. Stir in pasta sauce, savory, salt and pepper. Simmer, uncovered, for 10 minutes, stirring occasionally.

Toss lamb mixture with *hot* fusilli.

Makes 4 servings.

A SWEET NOTE

While the Italians have their share of lavish desserts, often a meal is ended on a light, sweet note. Here are two fresh and simple inspirations: Enjoy creamy ricotta cheese sprinkled with sugar, spooned into pretty ice cream dishes and topped with your choice of cocoa, cognac or fresh strawberries. Or, try fragrant melon balls sprinkled with Sicily's sweet Marsala wine and a few teaspoons of sugar, then chilled in the refrigerator for a few hours.

Asiago Polenta
with Mushroom Sauce

POLENTA CON ASIAGO AL SUGO DI FUNGHI

Asiago cheese lends its distinctively rich and nutty flavor to this traditional Italian side dish.

2 cups water	2 medium zucchini, halved lengthwise and sliced
¾ cup cornmeal	1 tablespoon olive oil
¾ cup cold water	1 (26-ounce) jar Classico® di Sicilia (Mushrooms & Ripe Olives) Pasta Sauce
¼ teaspoon salt	
½ cup freshly grated Asiago *or* Parmesan cheese	

For polenta, in medium saucepan, bring the 2 cups water to a boil. In small bowl, stir together cornmeal, the ¾ cup water and salt. Slowly add cornmeal mixture to boiling water, stirring constantly. Cook and stir until mixture returns to a boil. Reduce heat to very low. Cook, uncovered, about 5 minutes or until thick, stirring frequently. Stir in the Asiago or Parmesan cheese. Coat 8-inch square baking dish with vegetable cooking spray. Spread *hot* polenta in prepared dish; cool slightly. Cover; chill about 30 minutes or until firm.

Preheat oven to 350°. Bake polenta, uncovered, about 30 minutes or until hot. Remove from oven; let stand for 10 to 15 minutes.

Meanwhile, in large saucepan, over medium heat, cook zucchini in oil until tender-crisp, 3 to 4 minutes. Stir in pasta sauce; heat through.

To serve, unmold polenta onto cutting board. Cut polenta into 6 rectangles; cut each rectangle in half diagonally to form 12 triangles. Arrange 3 polenta triangles on each dinner plate; top with zucchini mixture.

Makes 4 side-dish servings.

VERSATILE POLENTA

Polenta is an Italian side dish that's often made simply with cornmeal and water. Sometimes served in place of pasta, polenta is enjoyed throughout Italy, with cooks adding their own regional ingredients for flavoring.

Asiago Polenta with Mushroom Sauce

Pasta Shapes and Sizes

Think of Italian cuisine and one of the first images that comes to mind is pasta. While long, thin strands of spaghetti have been much loved for decades in this country, today's cooks are beginning to appreciate the many shapes and sizes of this versatile food. With over 600 shapes and sizes of pasta available, these pointers will help you decide which to choose.

• Generally, pasta names ending in –*ini* designate smaller versions, while pasta names ending in –*oni* designate larger versions. For example, tortelloni is a larger version of tortellini and spaghettini is thinner than spaghetti.

• When choosing a long strand of pasta—capellini, spaghettini or spaghetti, remember that lighter, more delicate sauces such as Classico® di Napoli (Tomato & Basil) and Classico® di Parma (Four Cheese) Pasta Sauces go best with the thinner strands, while heartier and chunkier sauces such as Classico® di Toscana (Portobello Mushroom) and Classico® di Salerno (Roasted Peppers & Onion) Pasta Sauces are best suited to the thicker strands.

• Tubular pastas include rigatoni, mostaccioli and penne rigate. The more slender tubes (such as penne rigate) pair best with a tomato and cream sauce such as Classico® di Liguria (Tomato Alfredo) Pasta Sauce, while the larger tubes (such as rigatoni) are perfect for a hearty meat sauce such as Classico® d'Abruzzi (Italian Sausage & Fennel) Pasta Sauce.

• With their smooth surfaces, bow ties, linguine and fettuccine are well suited to a rich, creamy sauce.

Lasagna Rolls
with Eggplant and Prosciutto

CANNELLONI CON MELANZANE E PROSCIUTTO

If you can, seek out prosciutto di Parma *for this dish. It's one of the most cherished Italian cured hams.*

8   strips lasagna noodles, cooked as package directs, drained and rinsed with cold water

1   medium eggplant (about 1 pound), trimmed and peeled
    Olive oil for frying

1   (26-ounce) jar Classico® di Siena (Fire-Roasted Tomato & Garlic) Pasta Sauce

2   ounces thinly sliced prosciutto, chopped (optional)

1   (4-ounce) piece mozzarella cheese, cut into 8 sticks, *each* about 2½x½ inches

⅛   teaspoon pepper

¼   cup (1 ounce) shredded mozzarella cheese

Cut eggplant lengthwise into 8 slices, each about ¼ inch thick. In 12-inch skillet, over medium heat, cook 2 or 3 eggplant slices in oil until browned, 1 to 2 minutes on each side. Drain eggplant slices on paper towels. Repeat with remaining eggplant slices, adding more oil as needed.

Preheat oven to 400°. Pour *half* pasta sauce into 11x7-inch baking dish. To assemble lasagna roll, place an eggplant slice on a lasagna noodle. Top with some prosciutto and a stick of mozzarella cheese. Roll up lasagna noodle and eggplant around cheese and prosciutto (if desired). Place lasagna roll, seam-side down, on top of pasta sauce in baking dish. Repeat with remaining lasagna noodles, eggplant slices, prosciutto (if desired) and cheese sticks to make 8 rolls.

Sprinkle pepper over lasagna rolls. Spoon remaining pasta sauce over lasagna rolls. Cover tightly with foil; bake for 25 to 30 minutes or until sauce is bubbly and rolls are heated through.

To serve, place lasagna rolls on dinner plates; spoon sauce over lasagna rolls. Sprinkle with shredded cheese.

Makes 8 servings.

Penne with Vodka

PENNE ALLA VODKA

With its bacon and a Classico® Pasta Sauce rich in pecorino Romano cheese, this dish is reminiscent of spaghetti alla carbonara, a specialty of the Lazio region.

1   pound penne rigate, cooked as package directs and drained
4   *or* 5 slices bacon, finely chopped
1   onion, finely chopped
⅓   cup vodka *or* chicken broth
1   (26-ounce) jar Classico® di Palermo (Pecorino Romano & Herb) Pasta Sauce

⅓   cup whipping cream *or* evaporated skim milk
¼   cup chopped fresh parsley

In large saucepan, cook bacon 2 to 3 minutes. Add onion and cook until tender. Add vodka or broth; cook until liquid has reduced, about 1 minute. Stir in pasta sauce and cream; simmer for 4 to 5 minutes.

Toss sauce with *hot* penne rigate. Serve topped with parsley.

Makes 4 to 6 servings.

Italian
Fish Soup

ZUPPA DI PESCE

In Sicily, there are as many versions of this trattoria favorite as there are coastal towns. This soup gets its rich tomato flavor from Classico® di Napoli (Tomato & Basil) Pasta Sauce.

1 (14½-ounce) can chicken broth
1 (26-ounce) jar Classico® di Napoli (Tomato & Basil) Pasta Sauce
½ cup dry white wine

1 pound haddock, bass, sole *or* other fish fillets, rinsed and cut into chunks*
   Salt and pepper
4 slices Italian bread, toasted

In large saucepan, combine chicken broth, pasta sauce and wine. Bring to a boil; reduce heat. Simmer, uncovered, for 10 minutes.

Add fish to saucepan. Simmer about 5 minutes or until fish flakes easily when tested with a fork. Season to taste with salt and pepper.

To serve, ladle soup into bowls. Top with toasted Italian bread.

Makes 4 servings.

*If you like, substitute ¾ pound cooked crabmeat for the fish. Prepare as above, *except* just heat through after adding the crabmeat.

SAY PECORINO CHEESE

Pecorino cheese is a sharp-flavored sheep's-milk cheese that's been aged for 6 to 18 months. Though many regions in central and southern Italy make pecorino, the most well-known is pecorino Romano, which has a yellow rind and a creamy white center. Other varieties include pecorino Toscano and pecorino Siciliano. Classico® calls on pecorino cheese to lend distinctive flavor to its di Palermo (Pecorino Romano & Herb) Pasta Sauce.

Stuffed
Cabbage Rolls

INVOLTINI DI CAVOLO CON SALSICCIA

Next time you're serving rice for dinner, cook extra to get a jump start on this hearty one-dish meal for the next day's dinner.

¾ pound bulk Italian sausage *or* lean ground beef *or* ground raw turkey	1 cup cooked rice
½ cup chopped onion	8 medium to large green cabbage leaves
1 (26-ounce) jar Classico® di Palermo (Pecorino Romano & Herb) Pasta Sauce	

Preheat oven to 350°. For filling, in large skillet, over medium heat, cook Italian sausage and onion until meat is browned and onion is tender; pour off fat. Stir in *1 cup* pasta sauce and rice.

In large pot, bring 2 quarts water to a boil. Meanwhile, trim vein of *each* cabbage leaf even with edge of leaf. (Or, if desired remove center veins from cabbage leaves, keeping each leaf in 1 piece.) Immerse leaves, 4 at a time, into boiling water about 3 minutes or until limp. Drain well.

Place *about ⅓ cup* filling on *each* cabbage leaf. Fold in sides. Starting at an unfolded edge, carefully roll up each leaf, making sure folded sides are included in roll.

Pour *1 cup* pasta sauce into 8-inch square baking dish. Arrange cabbage rolls on top of sauce; top with remaining pasta sauce. Cover; bake for 30 to 35 minutes or until heated through.

Makes 4 servings.

Risotto
with Spinach and Herbs

RISOTTO CON SPINACI ALLE ERBE

Look for Arborio rice at large supermarkets or an Italian specialty store. The high starch content of this Italian-grown rice gives risotto its characteristic creamy texture.

2 tablespoons olive oil	Salt and pepper
1½ cups Arborio rice	½ teaspoon *each* dried basil leaves
5 to 6 cups chicken broth, heated	and dried thyme leaves
½ (26-ounce) jar Classico® di Firenze	Additional freshly grated
(Florentine Spinach & Cheese)	Parmesan cheese
Pasta Sauce	
3 tablespoons freshly grated	
Parmesan cheese	

In medium saucepan, over medium heat, cook rice in oil for 30 seconds, stirring constantly. Reduce heat to medium-low. Add ½ *cup* broth; cook, stirring constantly, until broth is absorbed. Add remaining broth, ½ *cup* at a time, stirring after each addition until broth is absorbed.

Stir in pasta sauce and the 3 tablespoons Parmesan cheese. Season to taste with salt and pepper. Sprinkle basil and thyme over risotto; serve with additional Parmesan cheese.

Makes 6 side-dish servings.

CLASSIC FLAVORS

Italian cooks have adored onions and garlic for centuries. Even today, many of Italy's masterful sauces begin with an expertly combined mixture of chopped onions, garlic and other vegetables and herbs sautéed in olive oil or butter. This essential first cooking step is called a soffritto.

Each Classico® Pasta Sauce carefully combines the best herbs and spices and uses the finest ingredients to bring you made-from-scratch taste.

Mushroom Ravioli
with Alfredo Sauce

RAVIOLI DI FUNGHI ALLA PANNA

This specialty is inspired by the region of Umbria, where the forests beckon mushroom hunters with their prized black truffles. Here, you may use your choice of fresh mushrooms for a simple substitute.

8 ounces fresh mushrooms (such as cremini, portobello, porcini or button), finely chopped (about 2⅔ cups)	⅔ cup part-skim ricotta cheese
	3 tablespoons freshly grated Asiago *or* Parmesan cheese
½ cup dry white wine *or* chicken broth	24 (3½-inch) wonton wrappers
1 tablespoon chopped fresh basil *or* ½ teaspoon dried basil leaves	1 tablespoon olive oil
	1 (26-ounce) jar Classico® di Liguria (Tomato Alfredo) Pasta Sauce
¼ teaspoon pepper	Chopped fresh parsley (optional)

In medium saucepan, combine mushrooms, wine or chicken broth, basil and pepper. Bring to a boil; reduce heat. Simmer, uncovered, for 15 to 20 minutes or until mushrooms are tender and no liquid remains. Remove from heat. Cool slightly.

For filling, stir together mushrooms, ricotta cheese and Asiago or Parmesan cheese. Place *scant tablespoon* filling in the center of *each* wonton wrapper. Brush edges of wrapper with water. Fold 1 corner over to the opposite corner, forming a triangle. To seal, press edges together with fingers.

Meanwhile, in large pot, bring 2 quarts water and the oil to a boil. Drop 6 ravioli into the boiling water. Cook, uncovered, about 2 minutes or until tender. Remove with a slotted spoon; drain on paper towels. Repeat with remaining ravioli, 6 at a time.

In medium saucepan, over medium-low heat, heat pasta sauce until warm. To serve, arrange 3 ravioli on each dinner plate. Top with sauce. Sprinkle with parsley if desired.

Makes 8 appetizer servings.

Bow Ties

with Artichoke Sauce

FARFALLE AL SUGO DI CARCIOFI

Italy grows more artichokes than any other country. It's said that the best come from Liguria—the region that inspired this inventive dish.

12 ounces bow ties, cooked as package directs and drained	Dash nutmeg
2 tablespoons butter	1 (14-ounce) can artichoke hearts, drained and cut up
1 tablespoon flour	1 cup seeded and chopped tomato
1½ cups half-and-half	1 tablespoon chopped fresh rosemary
½ cup freshly grated Parmesan cheese	*or* ½ to 1 teaspoon dried
⅛ teaspoon pepper	rosemary leaves, crumbled

In medium saucepan, melt butter; stir in flour. Gradually add half-and-half; mix well. Over low heat, cook and stir until slightly thickened. Stir in Parmesan cheese, pepper and nutmeg; heat through. Add artichoke hearts, tomato and rosemary. Simmer over low heat until hot, stirring occasionally. Toss with *hot* bow ties.

Makes 6 side-dish servings.

Bow Ties with Artichoke Sauce

Eggplant Parmigiana

Eggplant *Parmigiana*

MELANZANE ALLA PARMIGIANA
Parmigiana *in the name of this classic dish denotes its use of Parmesan cheese.*

Salt
2 large eggplants, sliced into
½-inch-thick rounds
Flour
Olive oil for frying
1 (26-ounce) jar Classico® di Parma
(Four Cheese) Pasta Sauce

1½ cups (6 ounces) shredded
mozzarella cheese
⅓ cup freshly grated Parmesan cheese
Additional freshly grated
Parmesan cheese

Lightly salt eggplant rounds and let stand for 60 to 90 minutes to draw out bitter juices; pat dry. Lightly toss eggplant in flour; remove and set aside.

In large skillet, over medium heat, heat *6 tablespoons* oil; fry eggplant rounds, 2 or 3 at a time, cooking until both sides are golden brown, adding more oil as necessary. Place cooked eggplant on paper towel-lined trays to absorb excess oil.

Spread a thin layer pasta sauce in 11x7-inch baking dish. Top with *one-third* eggplant, *one-third* pasta sauce, *half* mozzarella cheese and *one-third* of the ⅓ cup Parmesan cheese. Repeat layers, ending with eggplant. Top with remaining sauce and remaining Parmesan cheese. Bake, uncovered, for 25 to 30 minutes. Let stand 15 minutes before serving. Serve with additional Parmesan cheese if desired.

Makes 6 to 8 servings.

Lasagna Roll-Ups Florentine

CANNELLONI ALLA FIORENTINA

The inspiration for this dish straddles the border between Emilia-Romagna, known for its creamy dishes, and Tuscany, known for its use of spinach—designated by the word Fiorentina.

9 strips lasagna noodles, cooked as package directs and drained	1 (10-ounce) package frozen chopped spinach, thawed and well drained
2 tablespoons butter	1 cup (4 ounces) shredded mozzarella cheese
1 tablespoon flour	¼ cup freshly grated Parmesan cheese
1½ cups half-and-half	1 egg
½ cup freshly grated Parmesan cheese	Chopped fresh parsley (optional)
⅛ teaspoon pepper	
Dash nutmeg	
1 (15- *or* 16-ounce) container ricotta cheese	

In medium saucepan, melt butter; stir in flour. Gradually add half-and-half; mix well. Over low heat, cook and stir until slightly thickened. Stir in ½ cup Parmesan, pepper and nutmeg; heat through. Remove from heat; set aside.

Preheat oven to 350°. In medium bowl, combine ricotta, spinach, mozzarella, ¼ cup Parmesan and egg. Spread *about ⅓ cup* cheese mixture on *each* lasagna strip; roll up.

Pour *½ cup* sauce into bottom of 11x7-inch baking dish. Arrange lasagna rolls, seam-sides down, in dish; top with remaining sauce. Cover; bake about 35 minutes or until hot. Sprinkle with parsley if desired.

Makes 9 servings.

Lasagna Roll-Ups Florentine

Vegetable Calzones

CALZONE VEGETARIANO

Calzone means "pants" in Italian. Perhaps the cooks in Naples who invented this dish thought the stuffed turnovers looked like billowing trouser legs.

1 (16-ounce) loaf frozen bread dough, thawed

1 (26-ounce) jar Classico® di Parma (Four Cheese) Pasta Sauce

1 (14-ounce) can artichoke hearts, drained and coarsely chopped

1 (7¼-ounce) jar roasted red bell peppers, drained and coarsely chopped

1 (4-ounce) can sliced mushrooms, drained

1½ cups (6 ounces) shredded mozzarella cheese

2 tablespoons milk

4 teaspoons freshly grated Parmesan cheese

Preheat oven to 375°. Divide dough into 8 equal pieces; shape into balls. On lightly floured surface, roll each ball into a circle about 6 inches in diameter. Cover to prevent dough from drying out.

For filling, combine ¾ *cup* pasta sauce, artichoke hearts, roasted peppers and mushrooms. Spread *about* ⅓ *cup* filling evenly over *half of each* circle to within ½ inch of the edge. Sprinkle *3 tablespoons* mozzarella cheese over filling on *each* circle.

Moisten edge of each dough circle with water. Fold dough in half over filling. Seal edge by pressing with the tines of a fork. Prick tops. Lightly brush tops with milk; sprinkle with Parmesan cheese. Carefully place calzones 2 to 3 inches apart on greased baking sheets.

Bake about 20 minutes or until crust is lightly browned. Heat remaining pasta sauce; serve with calzones.

Makes 8 servings.

NOTE: Calzones may be prepared and baked as above, then frozen. To reheat, preheat oven to 375°. Place frozen calzones on baking sheet. Bake about 25 minutes or until heated through. If necessary, cover with aluminum foil the last 5 to 10 minutes of baking to prevent overbrowning.

Meatball *Panini*

PANINI CON POLPETTE

The Roman version of a fast-food lunch would be to enjoy a panini (or sandwich) while standing at the bar in the local café, where the glass cases brim with creative choices. This enjoyable sandwich reflects the spirit of the café-style panini.

1   egg, slightly beaten
¼   cup fine dry bread crumbs
2   tablespoons finely chopped onion
1   teaspoon fennel seed, crushed (optional)
1   pound ground beef *or* bulk pork sausage

1   (26-ounce) jar Classico® di Salerno (Roasted Peppers & Onion) Pasta Sauce
6   Italian rolls *or* bratwurst buns, split horizontally
¾   cup (3 ounces) shredded mozzarella cheese

Preheat oven to 400°. In medium bowl, stir together egg, bread crumbs, onion and fennel seed (if desired); add beef or pork and mix well. Shape into 24 meatballs. Place meatballs in shallow baking pan. Bake, uncovered, about 15 minutes or until meatballs are fully cooked. Drain on paper towels. In medium saucepan, bring pasta sauce to a boil. Gently stir in meatballs; heat through.

Hollow out bottom half of each roll, reserving bread crumbs for another use. Toast rolls (if desired) by broiling 3 to 4 inches from heat for 1 to 2 minutes. Spoon 4 meatballs and some sauce into the bottom half of each roll; sprinkle with cheese and top with roll top.

Makes 6 servings.

SHORTCUT MEATBALLS

To make a shortcut version of Meatball Panini or other meatball recipes, look for frozen prepared meatballs at your supermarket. Gourmet and specialty Italian food shops may also sell house-made versions. Smaller meatballs (about 1 inch) work best for this sandwich and for adding to casseroles, but when making that all-time favorite, spaghetti and meatballs, you may want to opt for a larger size.

Italian Sausage
Sandwiches

PANINI CON SALSICCIA

This dish salutes the Emilia-Romagna region of Italy, known for its many wonderful varieties of sausage.

¾ pound bulk Italian sausage *or* ground beef

1 (26-ounce) jar Classico® di Palermo (Pecorino Romano & Herb) Pasta Sauce *or* Classico® di Siena (Fire-Roasted Tomato & Garlic) Pasta Sauce

1 (4-ounce) can mushroom stems and pieces, drained

1 (16-ounce) loaf unsliced Italian bread (about 16x4 inches), split horizontally

6 ounces sliced mozzarella cheese

1 (7¼-ounce) jar roasted red bell peppers, drained and cut into ½-inch-wide strips

In large skillet, over medium-high heat, cook Italian sausage or ground beef until browned; pour off fat. Stir in pasta sauce and mushrooms. Bring to a boil; reduce heat. Simmer, uncovered, for 10 minutes.

Preheat oven to 375°. Hollow out bottom half of bread loaf, reserving bread crumbs for another use. Spoon meat mixture into hollowed-out bread. Arrange mozzarella cheese over top of meat mixture; top with red pepper strips.

Cover with loaf top. Place sandwich on baking sheet. Cover tightly with aluminum foil; bake about 15 minutes or until cheese melts and sandwich is heated through. Use serrated knife to cut loaf into 6 portions.

Make 6 servings.

Italian Sausage Sandwiches

Pizza Rustica

PIZZA RUSTICA

Pizzerias in Liguria are known for their stuffed versions of the pizza pie.
Try this satisfying version that begins with a hot roll mix.

1   (16-ounce) package hot
      roll mix
1   pound bulk Italian sausage
1   (26-ounce) jar Classico®
      di Salerno (Roasted Peppers
      & Onion) Pasta Sauce
1½ cups (6 ounces) shredded
      mozzarella cheese

1   (10-ounce) package frozen chopped
      spinach, thawed and well drained
1   egg, slightly beaten
      Milk to brush loaf
2   teaspoons sesame seed

Preheat oven to 350°. Prepare hot roll mix according to package directions
through the kneading step. Cover; let dough rest for 5 minutes.

Meanwhile, in large skillet, over medium-high heat, cook Italian sausage
until meat is browned; pour off fat. Stir in *1½ cups* pasta sauce; heat through.

Coat the bottom of a 9-inch springform pan* with vegetable cooking spray.
On lightly floured surface, roll *three-fourths* of the dough into 14-inch circle.
Fit into bottom and up side of prepared pan, allowing excess dough to
extend over edge of pan. Press pleats in dough as necessary to fit. Sprinkle
with *½ cup* mozzarella cheese. Spoon meat mixture over cheese. Combine
drained spinach, egg and remaining cheese; spread over meat mixture.

Roll remaining dough into 9-inch circle; place on top of spinach mixture.
Moisten edge of bottom crust with water; fold over edge of top crust to seal.
Brush top with milk; sprinkle with sesame seed.

Bake for 40 to 45 minutes or until crust is golden brown. Cool 10 minutes.

To serve, remove side of springform pan; cut pizza into wedges. Heat
remaining pasta sauce; serve over pizza.

Makes 8 servings.

*To use 13x9-inch baking pan, prepare as above except roll *three-fourths* of dough into
17x13-inch rectangle for bottom crust and roll remaining dough into 15x11-inch rectangle
for top crust.

Country Trad

A few riders stopping for a drink in the country
—*William Shakespeare's A Midsummer Night's Dream*

tions

Sea Bass with Tomato Pesto (recipe, page 40)

From terraced gardens, fertile croplands, dense woodlands and sparkling seas come Italy's bounty of cherished ingredients. Here, the hearty recipes celebrate the family-style dishes found in country homes throughout the abundant land.

Sea Bass

with Tomato Pesto

SPIGOLA CON SALSA DI POMODORO E PESTO

If sea bass is not available, substitute swordfish or halibut. Any of these mild-flavored fish blend deliciously with the authentic pesto flavor of Classico® di Genoa (Spicy Tomato & Pesto) Pasta Sauce. Pictured on page 39.

1 onion, finely chopped	¼ cup chopped fresh basil *or* parsley
2 cloves garlic, finely chopped	6 (1-inch-thick) sea bass fillets,
2 tablespoons olive oil	rinsed
½ cup dry white wine	
1 (26-ounce) jar Classico® di Genoa (Spicy Tomato & Pesto) Pasta Sauce	

Preheat oven to 400°. In medium saucepan, over medium heat, cook onion and garlic in oil until tender. Add wine; cook until most of the wine has evaporated, 1 to 2 minutes. Add pasta sauce and basil or parsley; heat through.

Spoon sauce into 13x9-inch baking dish. Arrange fish on top. Bake for 10 to 12 minutes or until fish flakes easily when tested with a fork. Serve fish with sauce.

Makes 6 servings.

FLAVOR WITH PESTO

Aromatic pesto has its origins in Genoa, a port city in the coastal region of Liguria. Legend has it that this bright green sauce—usually made with ground fresh basil, garlic, olive oil, Parmesan cheese and pine nuts—had an earthy freshness that the Genoese sailors yearned for on their long sea journeys. Today, Classico® adds a touch of this special flavor to its Classico® di Genoa (Spicy Tomato & Pesto) Pasta Sauce.

Pasta with Chicken and Sausage

PASTA CON POLLO E SALSICCIA

This dish's sumptuous pairing of chicken with the sausage in the pasta sauce is typical of a meal you might find in the Tuscan countryside.

- 8 ounces spaghetti, cooked as package directs and drained
- 1 pound skinned, boneless chicken breast halves, rinsed and cut into 1-inch pieces
- 2 teaspoons olive oil
- 1 small green bell pepper, cut into thin strips

- 1 (26-ounce) jar Classico® d'Abruzzi (Italian Sausage & Fennel) Pasta Sauce
- 2 teaspoons chopped fresh rosemary *or* ½ teaspoon dried rosemary leaves, crumbled

In large skillet, over medium heat, cook chicken in oil for 3 to 4 minutes or until chicken is fully cooked. Transfer chicken to a bowl, reserving drippings in skillet; set chicken aside.

In same skillet, over medium heat, cook green pepper strips until tender; pour off fat. Stir in pasta sauce and rosemary. Bring to a boil; reduce heat. Cover; simmer for 10 minutes, stirring occasionally. Add chicken; heat through.

Toss chicken mixture with *hot* spaghetti.

Makes 4 servings.

Steak

Italiano

PASTA CON CARNE E FUNGHI

This recipe is inspired by the country traditions in Tuscany's Chiani Valley, where Chianina cattle, the most prized beef source in Italy, are raised.

8   ounces penne rigate, cooked as package directs and drained
1   (¾-pound) round steak, cut in thin strips
½   cup chopped onion
1   (4-ounce) can mushroom stems and pieces, drained
2   cloves garlic, finely chopped
2   tablespoons olive oil
1   (26-ounce) jar Classico® di Toscana (Portobello Mushroom)
      Pasta Sauce
½   cup water
½   cup dry red wine
1   teaspoon Wyler's® beef-flavor bouillon granules
    Freshly shredded Parmesan cheese (optional)

In large skillet, over medium-high heat, cook and stir steak, onion, mushrooms and garlic in oil until steak is browned and vegetables are tender.

Add pasta sauce, water, wine and bouillon. Bring to a boil; reduce heat. Cover; simmer 20 minutes or until beef is tender.

Serve over *hot* penne rigate and top with Parmesan cheese if desired.

Makes 8 servings.

Steak Italiano

Shells

with Spicy Seafood Sauce

CONCHIGLIE CON FRUTTI DI MARE IN SALSA PICCANTE

This flavorful dish would be right at home in the countryside of Sicily, a Mediterranean island renowned for its spicy specialties and the array of seafood from its sparkling seas. Serve the dish with crusty bread to soak up the tasty sauce.

8 ounces medium shells, cooked as package directs and drained

1 (10-ounce) can whole baby clams

1 (26-ounce) jar Classico® di Roma Arrabbiata (Spicy Red Pepper) Pasta Sauce

1 tablespoon chopped fresh basil *or* 1 teaspoon dried basil leaves

¾ pound peeled and deveined raw shrimp

Freshly shredded Parmesan cheese

For sauce, drain clams, reserving juice; set clams aside. In large saucepan, combine the reserved clam juice, pasta sauce and basil. Bring to a boil; reduce heat. Cover; simmer for 10 minutes.

Stir in clams and shrimp. Return to boiling; reduce heat. Cover; simmer about 5 minutes or until shrimp are pink.

Toss clam mixture with *hot* shells. Sprinkle with Parmesan cheese.

Makes 4 servings.

Rigatoni
with Ham and Peas

RIGATONI CON PROSCIUTTO E PISELLI

Rigatoni, with its grooved tubular shape, is ideal for capturing lots of luscious Tomato Alfredo Pasta Sauce in every bite of this colorful Ligurian dish.

12 ounces rigatoni, cooked as package directs and drained
3   green onions, chopped
2   tablespoons olive oil
1   (26-ounce) jar Classico® di Liguria (Tomato Alfredo) Pasta Sauce

¼   pound medium-thick prosciutto slices, cut into strips, *or* smoked ham, diced
1   cup frozen peas
    Salt and pepper
    Chopped fresh parsley *or* basil

In large saucepan, over medium heat, cook green onions in oil for 2 to 3 minutes or until tender. Add pasta sauce, prosciutto or ham and peas; simmer 2 to 3 minutes or until heated through. Season to taste with salt and pepper. Toss prosciutto mixture with *hot* rigatoni. Sprinkle with parsley or basil.

Makes 4 servings.

SERVING PROSCIUTTO

Prosciutto *generally refers to ham that has been dry-cured for at least six months, resulting in a slightly sweet flavor. While it's often used in cooking—as in the above recipe—* prosciutto *is also enjoyed in sandwiches or as part of an antipasto platter. Try paper-thin slices wrapped around sweet balls of cantaloupe or peeled and quartered fresh figs.*

Pork Medallions Arrabbiata

Pork Medallions

Arrabbiata

LOMBATA DI MAIALE ALL'ARRABBIATA

The people of southern Italy's countryside often enjoy their dishes all'arrabbiata, which means "in the angry way"—with a healthy dose of spicy flavors. This dish gets those flavors from Classico₀ di Roma Arrabbiata (Spicy Red Pepper) Pasta Sauce.

8 ounces penne rigate, cooked as
    package directs and drained
1 medium onion, cut into wedges
½ *each* green and red bell peppers,
    cut into strips
2 tablespoons olive oil
1 (1-pound) pork tenderloin, cut into
    ½-inch-thick slices

2 cloves garlic, finely chopped
1 (26-ounce) jar Classico₀ di Roma
    Arrabbiata (Spicy Red Pepper)
    Pasta Sauce
¼ teaspoon dried thyme leaves

In large skillet, over medium heat, cook and stir onion and pepper strips in oil until tender; remove vegetables from skillet.

In same skillet, over high heat, cook pork and garlic until pork is browned on both sides, turning once. Add pasta sauce and thyme; simmer about 10 minutes or until pork is tender, stirring occasionally.

Add vegetables; heat through. Serve over *hot* penne rigate.

Makes 4 to 6 servings.

Shrimp
with Roasted Garlic Sauce

GAMBERETTI IN SALSA D'AGLIO ARROSTITO

Contrast the lively flavors of this southern Italian-style main dish with a cool and refreshing fruit sorbet for dessert.

8   ounces angel hair, cooked as
    package directs and drained
1   pound raw large shrimp, peeled
    and deveined
¼   cup chopped fresh basil
    or parsley

2   tablespoons olive oil
⅓   cup dry white wine
1½ cups Classico® di Sorrento
    (Roasted Garlic) Pasta Sauce
    Salt and pepper

In saucepan, over medium heat, cook shrimp and basil or parsley in oil for 2 to 3 minutes or until shrimp are pink. Add wine; cook until most of wine has evaporated, about 1 minute. Add pasta sauce; heat through. Season to taste with salt and pepper. Serve shrimp mixture over *hot* angel hair.

Makes 4 servings.

Creamy Linguine

with Smoked Salmon

LINGUINE CON SALMONE AFFUMICATO E PANNA

Although salmon is not native to their country, Italians enjoy the flavorful fish in many of their creations, such as this.

8 ounces linguine, cooked as package directs and drained	⅛ teaspoon pepper Dash nutmeg
2 tablespoons butter	6 ounces thinly sliced smoked salmon
1 tablespoon flour	¼ cup sliced green onions
1½ cups half-and-half	1 teaspoon finely shredded lemon peel
½ cup freshly grated Parmesan cheese	Chopped fresh parsley (optional)

In medium saucepan, melt butter; stir in flour. Gradually add half-and-half; mix well. Over low heat, cook and stir until slightly thickened. Stir in Parmesan cheese, pepper and nutmeg; heat through. Add salmon, green onions and lemon peel. Simmer, over low heat, until hot, stirring occasionally. Serve over *hot* linguine. Sprinkle with parsley if desired.

Makes 6 servings.

FRESH HERB HINTS

Purchase only as much fresh parsley or other fresh herbs as you can use in a few days. To store the herbs, trim the stems and place the sprigs, stems down, in about 2 inches of water in a tall plastic storage container or glass. Cover the leaves loosely with a plastic bag or plastic wrap; refrigerate for several days. An easy way to chop fresh herbs is to use kitchen scissors.

Soup

di Napoli

ZUPPA ALLA NAPOLETANA

Garbanzo beans are popular in soups throughout Italy. In this soup, they add a country-style robustness.

8   ounces medium shells, cooked as
    package directs and drained
½   pound Italian sausage links, sliced
1   small zucchini, sliced
    (about 1 cup)
1   small summer squash, sliced
    (about 1 cup)
½   cup chopped onion

3   cups water
1   (26-ounce) jar Classico® di Napoli
    (Tomato & Basil) Pasta Sauce
1   (16-ounce) can garbanzo beans,
    drained
1   tablespoon Wyler's® beef-flavor
    bouillon granules

In large pot, over medium-high heat, cook sausage until browned. Stir in zucchini, squash and onion; cook and stir until tender. Add all remaining ingredients except pasta. Bring to a boil; reduce heat. Cover; simmer 15 minutes. Stir in *hot* shells.

Makes 8 to 10 servings.

SOUP'S ON!

The general Italian word for soup is zuppa. However, the word used to describe a particular soup often depends on the soup's thickness. Minestra usually refers to a somewhat medium-thick meat and vegetable soup. Minestrina is a lighter soup that might begin a meal. And minestrone is a heartier, full-meal soup that often includes vegetables, pasta and beans.

Soup di Napoli

Spinach and Cheese
Stuffed Shells

(PICTURED ON FRONT COVER)

CONCHIGLIE RIPIENE DI SPINACI E FORMAGGIO

To add even more richness to this dish, use freshly grated Parmigiano Reggiano cheese, which is the true Parmesan cheese. Find it at an Italian specialty shop or deli counter—look for the words Parmigiano Reggiano stamped into the rind.

12 jumbo shells, cooked as package directs and drained
1 (10-ounce) package frozen chopped spinach, thawed and well drained
1 cup low-fat ricotta cheese
½ cup freshly grated Parmesan cheese

1 egg white, slightly beaten
2 tablespoons milk
1 (26-ounce) jar Classico® di Napoli (Tomato & Basil) Pasta Sauce
½ cup (2 ounces) shredded mozzarella cheese (optional)

Preheat oven to 350°. For filling, in small bowl, combine spinach, ricotta cheese, Parmesan cheese, egg white and milk. Stuff *each* shell with *about 2 tablespoons* filling.

Pour *about 1 cup* pasta sauce into an 8-inch square baking dish. Arrange stuffed shells in baking dish. Pour remaining sauce over shells. Cover; bake for 15 minutes. Uncover; bake about 15 minutes more or until heated through. Sprinkle with mozzarella cheese if desired; let stand 5 minutes.

Makes 4 servings.

Fusilli
with Artichoke Hearts

FUSILLI CON CUORI DI CARCIOFI

Italians prefer to toss their pasta with the sauce rather than topping it with the sauce. The Italian method works well in this recipe.

12	ounces fusilli, cooked as package directs and drained	1	(14-ounce) can artichoke hearts, drained and quartered
1	onion, finely chopped	¼	cup chopped fresh parsley
2	tablespoons olive oil		Salt and pepper
1	(26-ounce) jar Classico® di Sicilia (Mushrooms & Ripe Olives) Pasta Sauce		Freshly grated Parmesan *or* Romano cheese

In saucepan, over medium heat, cook onion in oil until tender. Add pasta sauce, artichoke hearts and parsley; simmer for 4 to 5 minutes or until heated through. Season to taste with salt and pepper. Toss artichoke mixture with *hot* fusilli and serve topped with Parmesan or Romano cheese.

Makes 4 servings.

SHAPED PASTA TO STUFF

The most common filled pastas include stuffed jumbo shells, ravioli, tortellini and its larger variation, tortelloni. Fillings for these often include cheeses and meats, but inventive chefs create other combinations that include stuffings of wild mushrooms, seafood, vegetables, winter squash and more. The exact origin of stuffed pasta is unknown; some say it was invented by thrifty servants of noblemen who filled pastas with ground ingredients left over from their employers' meals. Another legend claims that tortellini's round shape was inspired by the navel of a beautiful woman. Whatever their origin, the appeal of this inventive food endures.

Stuffed Peppers

di Capri

PEPERONI RIPIENI ALLA CAPRESE

There are many interpretations of stuffed peppers throughout Italy. This one hails from the ancient island of Capri, off the coast of Naples.

6 large red, yellow *or* green bell peppers	1 cup cooked rice
8 ounces fresh mushrooms, finely chopped	⅓ cup freshly grated Parmesan *or* Romano cheese
1 onion, finely chopped	¼ cup fine dry bread crumbs
¼ cup finely chopped fresh parsley	1 egg, slightly beaten
2 tablespoons olive oil	1 (26-ounce) jar Classico® di Capri (Sun-Dried Tomato) Pasta Sauce
1 pound lean ground veal, pork *or* beef	Salt and pepper

Preheat oven to 350°. Cut tops off peppers and set aside. Remove the seeds and membrane of each pepper.

In small saucepan, over medium heat, cook mushrooms, onion and parsley in oil until tender. Remove from heat. Combine cooked mushroom mixture with ground meat, rice, cheese, bread crumbs, egg and ¼ *cup* pasta sauce. Season with salt and pepper.

Spread remaining pasta sauce in 13x9-inch baking dish. Fill peppers with meat mixture and replace tops. Place peppers in prepared baking dish.

Cover; bake about 1 hour or until peppers are tender and meat is fully cooked. Serve peppers topped with sauce.

Makes 6 servings.

Lamb Chops and Cannellini

BRACIOLE DI AGNELLO E CANNELLINI

This simple one-dish meal features a favorite Italian ingredient—cannellini beans, also known as white kidney beans.

8 lamb rib chops, cut 1 inch thick and trimmed of fat	1 tablespoon balsamic vinegar
2 teaspoons olive oil	1 (19-ounce) can cannellini beans *or* 1 (16-ounce) can garbanzo beans, rinsed and drained
1 (26-ounce) jar Classico® di Salerno (Roasted Peppers & Onion) Pasta Sauce	2 tablespoons sliced pitted ripe olives
2 teaspoons chopped fresh rosemary *or* ¾ teaspoon dried rosemary, crumbled	Salt and pepper Fresh rosemary sprigs (optional)

In 12-inch skillet, over medium heat, cook chops in oil about 10 minutes for medium doneness, turning once. Transfer chops to plate, reserving drippings in skillet. Keep chops warm.

Stir pasta sauce, chopped or crumbled rosemary and vinegar into drippings in skillet. Bring to a boil; reduce heat. Simmer, uncovered, until sauce is thick, about 15 minutes. Stir in beans and olives. Top with chops; heat through. Season to taste with salt and pepper. Garnish with rosemary sprigs if desired.

Makes 4 servings.

THE OLIVE BRANCH

While the olive has been enjoyed for centuries throughout the Mediterranean, Italians have a special love affair with the fruit—they consume almost half of the olives grown annually in Europe. Italian markets brim with barrels of different shapes and hues of olives. In southern Italy, it's a sign of hospitality to welcome guests into one's home with an offering of bread and olives.

Roasted Vegetables
and Pasta di Siena

PASTA ALLA SENESE CON VERDURE ALLA GRIGLIA

Roasting is a technique well suited to the simple, rustic style of cooking so loved in the Tuscan countryside. This dish is named for the medieval hill town of Siena, which in ancient times was the region's capital.

8   ounces linguine, cooked as package directs and drained
1   small eggplant, cut in ½-inch-thick slices
1   medium zucchini, cut in half lengthwise
1   medium summer squash, cut in half lengthwise
1   medium onion, cut in thick slices
2   tablespoons olive oil
    Salt and pepper
1   (26-ounce) jar Classico® di Siena (Fire-Roasted Tomato & Garlic) Pasta Sauce
    Freshly shredded Asiago or Parmesan cheese (optional)

Preheat oven to 450°. Brush both sides of vegetable pieces with oil; sprinkle with salt and pepper. Arrange vegetables in single layer on lightly greased shallow baking pan. Bake for 10 minutes. Turn vegetables over; bake about 10 minutes more or until vegetables are lightly browned on both sides and tender. Cool and coarsely chop vegetables.

In large saucepan, heat pasta sauce; add vegetables. Heat through. Serve over *hot* linguine. Top with shredded cheese if desired.

Makes 6 servings.

Roasted Vegetables and Pasta di Siena

Rigatoni and Cheese
Casserole with Pesto

PASTICCIO DI RIGATONI E FORMAGGIO AL PESTO

Mozzarella was once a specialty of the Naples area, but master cheesemakers throughout southern Italy now produce the ever-popular cheese.

16 ounces rigatoni, cooked as package directs and drained

1 pound lean ground beef

2 (26-ounce) jars Classico® di Genoa (Spicy Tomato & Pesto) Pasta Sauce

1 (15- *or* 16-ounce) container ricotta cheese

4 cups (1 pound) shredded mozzarella cheese

¼ cup freshly shredded Parmesan cheese

2 eggs
    Additional freshly shredded Parmesan cheese
    Fresh basil

Preheat oven to 350°. In saucepan, over medium heat, cook beef until browned. Add pasta sauce. Cover; simmer 20 minutes.

In medium bowl, combine ricotta cheese, *1 cup* mozzarella cheese, the ¼ cup Parmesan cheese and eggs. Spread *1 cup* pasta sauce mixture on bottom of lightly greased 13x9-inch baking dish. Top with *half* cooked rigatoni, *half* ricotta cheese mixture and *half* remaining pasta sauce mixture. Sprinkle remaining mozzarella cheese over top. Repeat layering, ending with pasta sauce mixture.

Bake, uncovered, about 45 minutes or until hot and bubbly. Let stand for 15 minutes. Garnish with additional Parmesan cheese and fresh basil.

Makes 10 to 12 servings.

Venetian Chicken
in Spicy Cream Sauce

POLLO ALLA VENETA IN SALSA PICCANTE

The bountiful flat countryside around the city of Venice produces many rich ingredients, such as cream, which find their way into saucy dishes similar to this one.

1   pound penne rigate, cooked as package directs and drained
1   pound skinned, boneless chicken breasts, rinsed and cut into 1-inch pieces
3   tablespoons chopped fresh basil *or* 1 teaspoon dried basil leaves

2   tablespoons olive oil
1   (26-ounce) jar Classico® di Genoa (Spicy Tomato & Pesto) Pasta Sauce
½   cup whipping cream *or* evaporated skim milk
2   tablespoons chopped fresh parsley

In large skillet, over medium-high heat, cook and stir chicken and basil in oil until chicken is browned. Add pasta sauce, cream or evaporated milk and parsley. Bring to a boil; reduce heat. Cover; simmer about 10 minutes or until chicken is fully cooked. Serve over *hot* penne rigate.

Makes 4 to 6 servings.

SAVE THE JAR

Every time you purchase Classico® Pasta Sauce, you get a bonus—a sturdy jar. These jars are great for storing dried beans, cornmeal and popcorn in the kitchen; buttons and safety pins in the sewing room. They even make handy mugs for serving iced tea or water, and individual planters for herbs.

Spicy Chicken
and Penne Florentine

PENNE CON POLLO PICCANTE ALLA FIORENTINA

While the use of spinach (indicated by the word Fiorentina*)
recalls the city of Florence, the peppery flavors of this dish recall
a more southern Italian influence. The result is a great melding
of northern and southern styles.*

8   ounces penne rigate, cooked as package directs and drained
2   tablespoons flour
1   to 2 teaspoons pepper
1   teaspoon dried oregano leaves
4   skinned, boneless chicken breast halves (about 1 pound),
      rinsed
2   tablespoons olive oil
1   (26-ounce) jar Classico® di Firenze (Florentine Spinach
      & Cheese) Pasta Sauce
    Freshly shredded Parmesan cheese (optional)

In paper or plastic bag, combine flour, pepper and oregano.
Add chicken breast halves; shake to coat evenly.

In large skillet, over medium heat, cook chicken in oil until
fully cooked. Remove chicken; pour off fat.

Add pasta sauce to same skillet; cook until hot and bubbly.
Top with chicken. Cover; simmer 5 minutes.

Slice chicken; serve immediately over *hot* penne. Sprinkle
with Parmesan cheese if desired.

Makes 4 servings.

Spicy Chicken and Penne Florentine

Brunch

Frittata

FRITTATA

A frittata is an Italian-style omelet that's usually flipped out of the pan instead of being folded over. In this recipe, a springform pan allows you to skip the flipping step—simply remove the side of the pan to serve the frittata.

8   ounces vermicelli, cooked as
      package directs and drained
¾   cup (3 ounces) shredded Swiss
      cheese
1   medium tomato, chopped
½   cup chopped green bell pepper
½   cup sliced ripe olives
4   eggs, slightly beaten, *or* 1 (8-ounce)
      carton refrigerated egg substitute

½   cup freshly grated Parmesan cheese
¼   cup milk
1   teaspoon salt
⅛   teaspoon pepper
1   (26-ounce) jar Classico® di Salerno
      (Roasted Peppers & Onion) Pasta
      Sauce, heated

Preheat oven to 350°. Coat 9-inch springform or 9-inch round cake pan with vegetable cooking spray. Evenly distribute cooked pasta in pan. Sprinkle with Swiss cheese, tomato, green pepper and olives.

In small bowl, combine eggs, Parmesan cheese, milk, salt and pepper; mix well. Pour egg mixture over pasta mixture; press lightly to moisten pasta.

Cover with aluminum foil. Bake for 25 minutes. Uncover; bake for 20 minutes more. Serve warm topped with pasta sauce.

Makes 8 servings.

NOTE: Leftover cooked vermicelli may be used in this recipe. Cheddar, provolone or other favorite cheeses may be substituted for the Swiss cheese. Other vegetables may be substituted, such as chopped celery, onion, red bell pepper or green chilies.

Brunch Frittata

Vegetable and Bean Soup

MINESTRONE DI FAGIOLI

For a light lunch or supper, serve this full-flavored soup with thick slices of Italian bread topped with shredded mozzarella cheese and broiled to melt the cheese.

2 cups cubed zucchini

½ cup chopped carrot

1 tablespoon olive oil

2 cups shredded savoy *or* napa
   cabbage

1 (26-ounce) jar Classico®
   di Toscana (Portobello
   Mushroom) Pasta Sauce

1 (19-ounce) can cannellini beans *or*
   1 (16-ounce) can garbanzo beans,
   rinsed and drained

1 (14½-ounce) can beef broth

2 teaspoons chopped fresh rosemary
   or ½ teaspoon dried rosemary,
   crumbled

¼ teaspoon salt

In large saucepan, over medium heat, cook zucchini and carrot in oil about 3 minutes or until nearly tender; stir in cabbage. Cook about 1 minute more or until cabbage is tender, stirring constantly.

Stir in pasta sauce, beans, broth, rosemary and salt. Bring to a boil; reduce heat. Cover; simmer for 15 minutes.

Makes 6 side-dish servings.

The Herbs of Italy

It seems that Shakespeare was as enamored of herbs as the Italians, for references to the plants are sprinkled throughout his works. And just as herbs often have magical results in his plays, they also bring enchantment to Italian cooking. Here are a few favorites, and how they're used:

*"Fetch me this herb,
and be thou here again…"*
A Midsummer Night's Dream, II, i.

Basil, with a rich, mildly peppery flavor that suggests both mint and clove, is often used in pasta dishes or served fresh with white beans, tomatoes or mozzarella cheese. It's also a key ingredient in pesto sauce.

Fragrant sage has a slightly lemony, pungent, sometimes musty flavor that enhances roasted meats—especially poultry. It's also often used to add savory flavor to Italian pork sausage.

Another favorite Italian herb is the intensely fragrant oregano. Often used dried, it lends a pleasing pungency to stews and sauces.

*"And most, dear actors, eat no onions,
no garlic, for we are to utter sweet breath."*
A Midsummer Night's Dream, III, ii

While the actors in the wedding feast production are advised not to indulge in the sweet and mellow flavors of garlic, few Italian dishes go without this often-used ingredient. Garlic adds its delicious flavor to meat, fish, poultry, eggs and vegetables.

*"I know a bank where the wild thyme blows,
Where oxlips and the nodding violet grows…"*
A Midsummer Night's Dream, II, i

Thyme grows wildly throughout the Mediterranean region. The herb's strong, clovelike flavor complements many foods, including roasted poultry, fish, seafood and tomato-based sauces.

The Tuscan

Skillful cooks prepare favorite Italian dishes with ease
—*William Shakespeare's A Midsummer Night's Dream*

Table

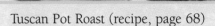

Tuscan Pot Roast (recipe, page 68)

Food-lovers everywhere are taking notice of Tuscany's celebrated cuisine, born of fresh, earthy ingredients prepared in simple yet discriminating ways. Experience these time-honored traditions with recipes that reflect the subtlety and grace of the Tuscan table.

Tuscan  Pot Roast

BRASATO ALLA TOSCANA

In Tuscany, this would be considered a special-occasion dish, because pastureland for raising cattle is scarce. Pictured on page 67.

1   2½- to 3-pound boneless beef chuck pot roast, trimmed of fat
2   tablespoons olive oil
1   (26-ounce) jar Classico® di Napoli (Tomato & Basil) Pasta Sauce
½   cup dry red wine
2   teaspoons Wyler's® beef-flavor bouillon granules

3   medium potatoes, quartered (1 pound)
4   medium carrots, cut into 2-inch-long pieces
2   small onions, cut into ½-inch-thick wedges
2   stalks celery, bias-sliced into 1-inch-long pieces

In large pot, over medium-high heat, brown roast on both sides in oil; pour off fat. Combine *1 cup* pasta sauce, wine and bouillon granules; pour over roast. Bring to a boil; reduce heat. Tightly cover; simmer for 1 hour.

Add potatoes, carrots, onions and celery to meat. Return to boiling; reduce heat. Cover; simmer for 45 to 60 minutes more or until meat and vegetables are tender, adding water if necessary.

Transfer meat and vegetables to serving platter, reserving *1 cup* juices; cover to keep warm. Add remaining pasta sauce to reserved juices in large pot. Bring to a boil; reduce heat. Simmer, uncovered, for 10 minutes. Spoon some of the sauce over the meat and vegetables; use remaining sauce as a condiment.

Makes 6 servings.

Crockery cooker method: Brown roast as above. In the bottom of 5- to 6-quart electric crockery cooker, layer roast, potatoes, carrots, onions and celery. Combine *1 cup* pasta sauce, wine and bouillon granules; pour over roast and vegetables. Cover; cook on low-heat setting for 9 to 11 hours or on high-heat setting for 4½ to 5½ hours or until meat and vegetables are tender.

Transfer meat and vegetables to serving platter; cover to keep warm. Reserve *1 cup* juices; discard any remaining juices. In medium saucepan, combine remaining pasta sauce and reserved juice. Bring to a boil. Serve as above.

Hearty Pasta
di Toscana

SPAGHETTI ALLA TOSCANA

For a fine complement to this filling dish, toss a simple green salad with a vinaigrette dressing made with balsamic vinegar, a favorite Italian ingredient.

- 8 ounces spaghetti, cooked as package directs and drained
- ½ pound ground turkey
- ½ cup chopped carrot
- ½ cup chopped onion
- 1 (26-ounce) jar Classico® di Toscana (Portobello Mushroom) Pasta Sauce
- 1 (19-ounce) can cannellini beans *or* 1 (16-ounce) can garbanzo beans, rinsed and drained
- Freshly grated Parmesan cheese (optional)

In large skillet, over medium-high heat, cook turkey until browned. Add carrot and onion; cook and stir until vegetables are tender. Add pasta sauce and beans; simmer about 10 minutes or until heated through. Serve over *hot* spaghetti. Sprinkle with Parmesan cheese if desired.

Makes 8 servings.

PASTA SAUCE TO THE RESCUE

For a quick-to-fix snack, spread a little Classico® Pasta Sauce on an English muffin half or flour tortilla; sprinkle with shredded cheese and broil. Or, heat the pasta sauce and serve it as a dipping sauce with baked pizza snacks, soft pretzels, breadsticks or tortillas. For a special brunch or supper dish, top scrambled eggs with heated pasta sauce. Or, set up a baked potato bar with plenty of cooked ground beef, shredded cheese, chopped onion and heated pasta sauce.

Chicken
with Olives

POLLO CON LE OLIVE

Olive groves add beauty and grace to the Tuscan landscape, and their fruit adds color and spark to dishes, such as this one.

8 ounces spinach fettuccine, cooked as package directs and drained

8 medium chicken thighs (about 2½ pounds), skinned if desired and rinsed, *or* 4 skinned, boneless chicken breast halves, rinsed

2 tablespoons olive oil
Salt and pepper

1 (26-ounce) jar Classico® di Sorrento (Roasted Garlic) Pasta Sauce

½ cup sliced pimiento-stuffed olives
Chopped fresh parsley (optional)

In 12-inch skillet, over medium heat, cook chicken in oil until lightly browned, about 15 minutes, turning to brown evenly. Sprinkle with salt and pepper. Remove chicken from skillet; set aside. Pour off fat.

In same skillet, combine pasta sauce and olives in skillet. Bring to a boil. Return chicken to skillet. Reduce heat to low. Cover; simmer about 30 minutes or until chicken is fully cooked.

Serve chicken and sauce over *hot* fettuccine. Sprinkle with parsley if desired.

Makes 4 servings.

Garlic-Roasted
Chicken Breasts

PETTI DI POLLO ARROSTO ALL'AGLIO

In Tuscany, chicken is most often prepared on a spit or roasted in the oven; the latter is a perfect method for melding the mellow flavors of this dish.

8 ounces bow ties, cooked as package directs and drained	1 tablespoon lemon juice
	2 teaspoons olive oil
4 large chicken breast halves (about 2½ pounds total), skinned if desired and rinsed	1 teaspoon dried sage leaves
	1 (26-ounce) jar Classico® di Sorrento (Roasted Garlic) Pasta Sauce

Preheat oven to 425°. Place chicken breast halves, bone sides down, in a lightly greased 15x10-inch baking pan. Combine lemon juice, oil and sage; brush on the chicken breast halves.

Bake for 30 to 35 minutes or until chicken is fully cooked.

In small saucepan, over medium heat, heat pasta sauce until hot. Toss pasta sauce with *hot* bow ties. Serve chicken breasts on top of pasta.

Makes 4 servings.

A TASTE OF TUSCANY

The food of Tuscany is simply prepared. Rather than the rich sauces favored by their neighbors in the Emilia-Romagna region to the north, Tuscans prefer well-chosen ingredients at their height of freshness, often serving them unadorned, except for a drizzle of locally produced olive oil and perhaps a sprinkling of herbs. Meats are often grilled over charcoal. While Tuscans may be derided by other Italians for their love of dried beans, Tuscan cooks have raised the lowly legume to delicious heights in their soups, stews, pasta dishes and side dishes.

No-Boil
Classic Lasagna

LASAGNE CLASSICHE SENZA BOLLITURA

Skip a step! This Florentine-style dish is made even easier, because you don't need to boil the noodles.

8 ounces lasagna noodles, uncooked

1 (15- *or* 16-ounce) container
ricotta cheese

½ cup freshly grated Parmesan cheese

2 eggs, slightly beaten

2 (26-ounce) jars Classico® di Firenze
(Florentine Spinach & Cheese)
Pasta Sauce*

1 pound bulk Italian sausage, cooked
and drained

2 cups (8 ounces) shredded
mozzarella cheese

Preheat oven to 350°. In medium bowl, combine ricotta cheese, Parmesan cheese and eggs; mix well. In 13x9-inch baking dish, spread *1 cup* pasta sauce. Layer with *half each* uncooked lasagna noodles, ricotta cheese mixture, sausage, remaining pasta sauce and mozzarella cheese. Repeat layering.

Cover tightly with aluminum foil; bake for 1 hour. Uncover; bake 15 minutes more or until hot and bubbly. Let stand about 15 minutes before serving.

Makes 9 to 12 servings.

*You may substitute Classico® di Napoli (Tomato & Basil) Pasta Sauce for the Classico® di Firenze (Florentine Spinach & Cheese) Pasta Sauce.

THE FLORENTINE STYLE

The term florentine, *French for "in the style of Florence," has illustrious connections to that city. In the 16th century, Catherine de Medici, of a famed Florentine family, married the King of France. She brought her personal chefs with her to France, and it was there that they first encountered fresh spinach. Legend has it they were so impressed by the vegetable that anything containing spinach took on the name of their celebrated Renaissance city.*

No-Boil Classic Lasagna

Rotini Puttanesca

Rotini
Puttanesca

ROTINI ALLA PUTTANESCA

Puttanesca *is a classic Italian sauce made with tomatoes, capers and oregano.*

- 8 ounces rotini, cooked as package direct and drained
- 1 (26-ounce) jar Classico® di Roma Arrabbiata (Spicy Red Pepper) Pasta Sauce
- ½ cup shredded carrot
- 1 tablespoon capers, drained
- 1 tablespoon chopped fresh oregano *or* 1 teaspoon dried oregano leaves

  Crushed red pepper (optional)

  Freshly grated Parmesan cheese (optional)

In large saucepan, combine pasta sauce, carrot, capers, oregano and (if desired) red pepper. Bring to a boil; reduce heat. Cover; simmer for 15 minutes, stirring occasionally.

Toss sauce with *hot* rotini. Sprinkle with Parmesan cheese if desired.

Makes 4 side-dish servings.

Fettuccine

with Shrimp and Mussels

FETTUCCINE CON GAMBERI E COZZE

Italians enjoy wine—not only for drinking, but for cooking as well. Adding wine to the pot brings a distinctive aroma and flavor to the dish, as this recipe demonstrates.

12 ounces fettuccine, cooked as package directs and drained

½ pound raw large shrimp, peeled and deveined

2 tablespoons olive oil

1 onion, finely chopped

3 cloves garlic, finely chopped

½ cup dry white wine

1 (26-ounce) jar Classico® di Napoli (Tomato & Basil) Pasta Sauce

1 pound mussels, cleaned*

¼ cup chopped fresh parsley

Salt and pepper

Chopped fresh parsley (optional)

In large pot, over medium heat, cook shrimp in oil 3 to 4 minutes or until pink. Remove shrimp; set aside. Add onion and garlic to large pot; cook until tender. Add wine; cook until most of the wine has evaporated. Add pasta sauce and mussels. Cover; simmer 5 to 7 minutes or until mussels open.

Return shrimp to large pot; heat through. Stir in the ¼ cup parsley; season to taste with salt and pepper. Toss seafood mixture with *hot* fettuccine; serve topped with additional parsley if desired.

Makes 4 to 6 servings.

*When buying mussels in the shell, select those that are tightly closed, moist and unchipped. To clean the mussels, rinse them under cold, running water while scrubbing with a stiff-bristled brush. Remove the beard (the "hairy" part that you'll see between the two halves of the shell) of each mussel by grasping it and pulling firmly to remove it.

Fettuccine with Shrimp and Mussels

Prosciutto- and Sage-Stuffed
Chicken Rolls

INVOLTINI DI POLLO E PROSCIUTTO ALLA SALVIA

Tuscans so enjoy sage that the larger leaves are sometimes served battered and fried. Here, the earthy herb pairs perfectly with chicken.

8 ounces spinach fettuccine, linguine *or* spaghetti, cooked as package directs and drained
⅓ cup fine dry bread crumbs
⅓ cup finely shredded carrot
2 tablespoons water
2 tablespoons pine nuts
1 tablespoon chopped fresh sage *or* ½ teaspoon dried sage leaves

4 large boned, skinless chicken breast halves (about 1½ pounds), rinsed
4 thin slices prosciutto
1 tablespoon olive oil
1 (26-ounce) jar Classico® di Liguria (Tomato Alfredo) Pasta Sauce

For filling, in small bowl, combine bread crumbs, carrot, water, pine nuts and sage; set aside.

Place each chicken breast half, boned side up, between 2 pieces plastic wrap. With flat side of mallet and working from center to edges, pound lightly to form ⅛-inch-thick rectangle. Remove plastic wrap.

For each chicken roll, lay a prosciutto slice on top of a chicken breast; top with *about 2 rounded tablespoons* filling. Roll up from short side. Secure with wooden toothpicks or tie with 100% cotton string. In large skillet, over medium-high heat, cook chicken rolls in oil until browned on all sides; pour off fat.

Add pasta sauce to skillet. Bring to a boil; reduce heat. Cover; simmer about 15 minutes or until chicken is fully cooked. Remove toothpicks or string.

Serve chicken rolls and sauce over *hot* pasta.

Makes 4 servings.

Veal Stew

SPEZZATINO DI VITELLO

This hearty stew features veal, one of Tuscany's most popular meats.

1½	pounds veal stew meat, cut into 1-inch cubes	¼	cup dry red wine
1	tablespoon olive oil	2	cups cubed potatoes
1	(26-ounce) jar Classico® di Napoli (Tomato & Basil) Pasta Sauce	1	cup sliced carrots
1	(14½-ounce) can beef broth	1	medium onion, cut into thin wedges
		1¼	cups thinly sliced zucchini

In large pot, over medium-high heat, cook meat, *half* at a time, in oil until browned; pour off fat. Return all meat to pan; add pasta sauce, beef broth and wine. Stir in potatoes, carrots and onion. Bring to a boil; reduce heat. Cover; simmer for 45 minutes.

Stir in zucchini. Return to boiling; reduce heat. Cover; simmer about 15 minutes more or until meat and vegetables are tender.

Makes 6 servings.

FROM BREAD TO BRUSCHETTA

Bruschetta—the Italian version of garlic bread—is the rage in restaurants across America. Rather than being served with the main course, bruschetta is traditionally served as an appetizer. To make a classic bruschetta, simply grill or broil hearty slices of country bread (Italians often grill it over coals). Rub the slices with a peeled, cut garlic clove and brush with olive oil. If you like, garnish with sliced fresh tomatoes and herbs.

Capellini
Fritters

FRITTATINE DI CAPELLINI

These delicately fried fritters take on the robust flavor of whatever Classico® Pasta Sauce you serve with them. They make a scrumptious light supper or appetizer.

8   ounces capellini, broken into fourths, cooked as package directs and drained

3   eggs

¼   cup freshly grated pecorino Romano *or* Parmesan cheese

½   teaspoon freshly ground black pepper

Olive oil

Classico® Pasta Sauce, any flavor, heated

In medium bowl, beat eggs with Romano or Parmesan cheese and pepper; stir in cooked capellini.

In nonstick skillet, over medium heat, heat *2 tablespoons* oil. For *each* fritter, drop ¼ *cup* capellini mixture into skillet; press down slightly. Cook until lightly browned on both sides. Drain on paper towels. Repeat with remaining capellini mixture, adding more oil as necessary. Serve fritters warm with pasta sauce.

Makes 12 to 14 fritters.

SERVING OLIVE OIL

Olive oil is such a popular condiment in Tuscany that in some restaurants there, a bottle of it will be placed on the table next to salt and pepper for drizzling over such dishes as bruschetta, mozzarella and tomato salad, soups and meats. While most areas of Italy produce their own varieties, the Tuscan olive oil is characteristically dark, intensely flavored and aromatic. To serve olive oil for drizzling, choose extra-virgin olive oil. However, because extra-virgin olive oil is costly and loses it rich character upon heating, less-expensive virgin or pure olive oil are better choices for cooking.

Capellini Fritters

Spinach
Gnocchi

GNOCCHI DI SPINACI

In Tuscany, oblong-shaped gnocchi are often called topini *or "little mice."*

1 (10-ounce) package frozen spinach, thawed and well drained
1 egg, slightly beaten
1 cup mashed potatoes (without butter and salt)
¾ cup soft bread crumbs
⅔ cup flour
¼ cup finely chopped onion
¼ cup freshly grated Parmesan cheese
⅛ teaspoon pepper
1 (26-ounce) jar Classico® di Parma (Four Cheese) Pasta Sauce, heated

In medium bowl, combine spinach and egg. Add potatoes, bread crumbs, flour, onion, Parmesan cheese and pepper, stirring until mixture sticks together.

Divide spinach mixture into quarters. Shape each quarter into a log 15 inches long; cut each log into 1-inch-long pieces. Roll pieces lightly in additional flour to prevent sticking, if necessary.

In large saucepan, bring large amount of lightly salted water to a boil; add *half* gnocchi pieces and cook for 1 to 2 minutes or until gnocchi have risen to the top. Using slotted spoon, remove gnocchi; keep warm. Repeat with remaining gnocchi pieces. Serve sauce over gnocchi.

Makes 5 side-dish servings.

LITTLE DUMPLINGS

Gnocchi is the generic Italian word for dumplings. While the above recipe features the Tuscan hallmark of spinach, gnocchi are enjoyed throughout Italy in a variety of ways. Roman cooks often make their gnocchi with semolina, while the cooks of Venice often use potatoes for the dough and dress them with butter and smoked ricotta.

The Wines of Italy

One quarter of the world's wine hails from Italy, where the climate and soil are well suited to vineyards and the lifestyle is well suited to enjoying wine. Though the regions of Piedmont, Tuscany and Veneto produce the most wine, each region of the country prizes its own varieties. Here are a few of the well-known Italian wines:

Red Wines

Chianti, made in the Tuscan region of Chianti, is probably Italy's most famous red wine. Its dry, fruity appeal makes it a fine choice with the simple, earthy foods so loved in the area. While the wine was traditionally bottled in bulb-shaped bottles encased by straw, today's better Chianti are sold in the classic (Bordeaux-style) bottles. Look for the designation "Chianti Classico" or the higher-quality "Chianti Classico Riserva."

From Veneto, near Verona (the city of Romeo and Juliet), hails *Bardolino,* a light red wine with a delicate, dry flavor. Made from a blend of three grapes, the wine is best enjoyed while young and goes well with fish, veal and poultry.

Meat, game, strong cheeses and other robust-flavored foods call for *Barolo,* produced in northern Italy's Piedmont region from the Nebbiolo grape. This complex wine has a smooth, deep flavor.

Barbaresco, also from Piedmont, is full-bodied, yet less complex than Barolo. This red wine goes well with beef, veal and cheeses.

White Wines

Soave, a dry white wine from Veneto, has a mild, delicate flavor. Enjoy it chilled with antipasto, fish or poultry.

From the Lazio and Umbria regions comes *Orvieto,* a fruity white wine that can be dry or semi-sweet. Try it with antipasto or dessert.

Verdicchio, a dry white wine of east-central Italy, has a fresh flavor that tastes great with fish.

Sparkling and Dessert Wines

Marsala is considered one of Sicily's greatest gifts to the world of wine. The amber, sherry-like wine, available both sweet and dry, makes a luscious aperitif or a fine finale.

Toast the conclusion of a great meal with a glass of sparkling *Asti Spumante* from the Piedmont region.

The Wedding

Adults and children enjoying the lavish Wedding Feast
—William Shakespeare's *A Midsummer Night's Dream*

Feast

Lemon-and-Herb Roasted Chicken (recipe, page 89) and Roasted Potatoes (recipe, page 90)

A highlight of "William Shakespeare's A Midsummer Night's Dream" is the lavish Wedding Feast. For your next dinner party, share the tradition of a true Italian feast by treating your friends to a luscious six-course spread inspired by this sumptuous celebration.

Traditional Italian meals, like this Wedding Feast, often consist of four to six courses, beginning with *antipasto*. The next course or *primo piatto*, is usually pasta, rice/risotto or soup. Next comes the *secondo piatto* of meat or fish, served with or followed by the *insalata* or salad. Diners then often linger over fresh fruit and cheese, followed by a sweet or *i dolci*. Today most Italians eat this way only on special occasions and often are turning the *primo piatto* or pasta course into the dinner's main entrée.

Antipasto
Grilled Sausages with Pepper-Onion Sauté
Baked Mostaccioli or Meatball Soup
Lemon-and-Herb Roasted Chicken
with Roasted Potatoes
Mixed greens salad with vinaigrette dressing
Italian Wedding Cake and assorted Italian cookies

You won't need a royal kitchen staff to expertly prepare this inspired meal. Just follow this step-by-step plan and you'll pull off this feast with ease.

1 Day Ahead
- Bake layers for Italian Wedding Cake; cool, cover and store at room temperature.
- Prepare Baked Mostaccioli or Meatball Soup (without spinach); refrigerate.
- Cook and grill sausages for Grilled Sausages with Pepper-Onion Sauté; refrigerate.

4 Hours Ahead
- Wash and sort greens for salad.
- Prepare your favorite vinaigrette salad dressing.
- Arrange packaged or homemade cookies on platter.

2 Hours Ahead
- Prepare Lemon-and-Herb Roasted Chicken; roast.
- Assemble Roasted Potatoes; set aside.
- Assemble Italian Wedding Cake.

1 Hour Ahead
- Finish preparing Grilled Sausages with Pepper-Onion Sauté.
- Assemble Antipasto.

30 Minutes Ahead
- Reheat Baked Mostaccioli or bring Meatball Soup to boil; add spinach and cook until wilted.
- Roast potatoes.

Grilled Sausages

with Pepper-Onion Sauté

SALSICCIA ALLA GRIGLIA CON PEPERONI E CIPOLLE

*If you like, serve this dish as part of the antipasto course for the Wedding Feast.
(See tip, page 89.)*

2 pounds sweet *or* hot fresh Italian sausage links	2 medium green bell peppers, cut into thin slices
3 cups water	2 medium red bell peppers, cut into thin slices
2 onions, sliced and separated into rings	2 tablespoons olive oil

Pierce sausages with fork. In large saucepan, combine sausage links and water. Bring to a boil; reduce heat. Cover and simmer about 10 minutes or until sausage links are fully cooked; drain.

In large skillet, over medium heat, cook onion and bell peppers in oil for 5 to 7 minutes or until tender and lightly browned. Remove from heat; keep warm.

Grill sausages on rack of an uncovered grill directly over medium coals for 7 to 8 minutes or until skins are golden, turning often.* Diagonally slice sausages into thirds.

Add sausage pieces to vegetables in skillet; heat through for 1 to 2 minutes.

Makes 8 to 10 servings.

*To brown sausages on the rangetop rather than on the grill: In skillet, over medium heat, fry sausages in 1 tablespoon olive oil until browned. Remove from skillet. Diagonally slice sausage links into thirds. Continue as above.

Meatball Soup

ZUPPA CON POLPETTINE

This well-seasoned soup, served with thick slices of country Italian bread and a salad, makes a great light supper.

1 egg, beaten	1 cup water
½ cup soft bread crumbs	1 teaspoon dried Italian seasoning, crushed
3 tablespoons freshly grated Romano *or* Parmesan cheese	⅛ to ¼ teaspoon pepper
1 tablespoon finely chopped onion	¼ cup anelli (little rings), uncooked
½ pound lean ground beef	2 cups torn fresh spinach
2 (14½-ounce) cans beef broth	

Preheat oven to 350°. In medium bowl, stir together egg, bread crumbs, Romano or Parmesan cheese and onion; add ground beef and mix well. Shape meat mixture into 32 balls. Arrange meatballs in a 15x10-inch baking pan. Bake for 15 minutes or until no pink remains in centers of meatballs.

Meanwhile, in large pot, combine beef broth, water, Italian seasoning and pepper. Bring to a boil. Stir in anelli. Reduce heat. Cover; simmer about 8 minutes or until anelli is tender. Stir in meatballs; heat through.

Add spinach and cook for 1 to 2 minutes more or just until spinach is wilted.

Makes 8 to 10 servings.

Lemon-and-Herb Roasted Chicken

POLLO ARROSTO AL LIMONE E ALLE ERBE

The flavorful combination of lemon, garlic and dried herbs transforms simple roasted chicken into an elegant dish. Pictured on page 85.

1 medium lemon	1 teaspoon dried basil leaves
1 tablespoon olive oil	1 teaspoon dried rosemary leaves, crumbled
1 5- to 6-pound roasting chicken, rinsed	½ teaspoon salt
2 cloves garlic, finely chopped	½ teaspoon ground sage

Preheat oven to 375°. Halve lemon; squeeze *2 tablespoons* lemon juice from the lemon. Reserve lemon halves. Stir together oil and lemon juice. Brush chicken with oil mixture. In small bowl, combine garlic, basil, rosemary, salt and sage; rub onto chicken. Place the squeezed lemon halves in body cavity of chicken.

If desired skewer neck skin to back; tie legs to tail and twist wing tips under back. Place chicken, breast side up, on rack in shallow roasting pan.

Roast, uncovered, for 1½ to 1¾ hours or until chicken is no longer pink next to bone on inner thigh. Cover; let stand 10 minutes before carving.

Makes 8 to 12 servings.

ANTIPASTO IDEAS

Many Americans believe the word antipasto *means "before the pasta," but the word actually means "before the meal," as* pasto *is the Italian word for "meal."*

Culinary quibbles aside, here are some ideas for the Wedding Feast antipasto: Select a variety of Italian specialty meats and cheeses. Set out bowls of ripe and green olives, marinated artichoke hearts and roasted red bell peppers. Add an array of fruits, such as figs, melon balls and strawberries, to complement the savory foods.

Baked Mostaccioli

MOSTACCIOLI AL FORNO

Serve this Italian style as the first main course.

12 ounces mostaccioli, cooked as package directs and drained

1 (26-ounce) jar Classico® di Sicilia (Mushrooms & Ripe Olives) Pasta Sauce

1 cup (4 ounces) shredded mozzarella cheese

½ (3½-ounce) package sliced pepperoni, chopped

1 to 2 tablespoons chopped pepperoncini salad peppers

¼ teaspoon pepper

Preheat oven to 375°. In large bowl, combine *hot* mostaccioli, pasta sauce, *half* mozzarella cheese, pepperoni, salad peppers and pepper.

Spoon into 2-quart casserole; cover.* Bake for 20 minutes. Uncover; sprinkle with remaining cheese. Bake for 5 to 10 minutes more or until heated through.

Makes 8 to 12 servings.

*If desired, store in the refrigerator overnight. To reheat, preheat oven to 375°. Bake, covered, for 35 minutes. Uncover; sprinkle with remaining cheese. Bake 5 to 10 minutes more or until heated through.

Roasted Potatoes

PATATE ARROSTITE

Not only are these potatoes tasty with chicken, they're delicious with roast beef or pork, too. Pictured on page 85.

2½ pounds medium round red potatoes, quartered

2 tablespoons olive oil

1 teaspoon dried basil leaves

¼ teaspoon dried rosemary leaves, crumbled

¼ teaspoon coarsely ground black pepper

Preheat oven to 375°. In covered saucepan, cook potatoes in boiling lightly salted water for 5 minutes; drain well. Place potatoes in greased 11x7-inch baking dish. Combine remaining ingredients. Drizzle over potatoes; toss gently.

Bake for 25 to 30 minutes or until potatoes are tender and brown on edges, stirring once.

Makes 8 to 10 side-dish servings.

Italian
Wedding Cake

TORTA NUZIALE ITALIANA

Be sure to present this cake whole before cutting it, so your guests can appreciate your masterpiece in its entirety. Pictured on page 93.

1⅓	cups flour	⅔	cup milk
¼	cup ground almonds	3	tablespoons butter
1½	teaspoons baking powder	4	tablespoons dark rum
⅛	teaspoon salt	2	(12-ounce) jars apricot preserves
3	eggs		Assorted sliced fresh fruit
1½	cups sugar		(see photo, page 93)

Preheat oven to 325°. Grease bottom of two 8-inch round cake pans and one 10-inch springform pan or 10-inch round cake pan. Line bottoms with waxed paper; grease and flour waxed paper. Set aside.

Do not double the batter. In bowl, combine flour, ground almonds, baking powder and salt; set aside. In large bowl, use electric mixer on high speed to beat eggs about 5 minutes or until thick and lemon colored. Gradually add sugar, beating on medium speed about 5 minutes or until sugar is almost dissolved. Add flour mixture; beat on low to medium speed until combined.

In small saucepan, over low heat, heat milk and butter just until butter melts. Stir in *2 tablespoons* rum. Stir warm milk mixture into beaten egg mixture.

Divide batter evenly between prepared 8-inch round pans. Bake 30 to 35 minutes or until cakes spring back when lightly touched in center. On wire racks, cool in pans 10 minutes. Loosen sides of cakes from pans; remove cakes from pans. Carefully peel off waxed paper. On wire racks, cool completely.

Prepare a second batch of cake batter as above. Spoon batter into prepared 10-inch pan. Bake for 35 to 40 minutes or until cake springs back when touched lightly in center. Cool and remove from pan as above.

For apricot glaze, in small saucepan, combine preserves and remaining rum; heat and stir until just melted; cool slightly. Transfer to blender container or food processor; cover and blend or process until smooth.

Assemble cake as directed in tip on page 92.

Makes 24 servings.

Assembling the Italian Wedding Cake

Putting together a tiered cake isn't difficult but it does take some time and patience. Start by gathering the materials you'll need: Long serrated knife, large round cake board or flat platter (14 to 16 inches in diameter), 8-inch cardboard cake circle covered with aluminum foil, wooden dowel ($3/16$ to $1/4$ inch in diameter) and heavy scissors or small saw to cut dowel.

To assemble the cake, use the long serrated knife to trim off rounded tops of cooled cake layers. Place the 10-inch cake layer on the cake board or platter. Brush top of cake layer with some of the apricot glaze (part of cake recipe, page 91). Place an 8-inch cake layer, cut side up, on the foil-covered cake circle. Brush top of cake layer with more of the apricot glaze; reserve remaining apricot glaze for decorating cake. Stack the second 8-inch cake layer, cut side down, on top of the 8-inch layer on cake circle.

To provide support for the top cake tier, cut and position dowel pieces. First, measure height of 10-inch cake; use the scissors or small saw to cut 4 dowels this height, making sure all 4 dowels are exactly the same length. Then, place a dowel piece, cut end down, about 2 inches from edge of 10-inch cake; gently push dowel into cake until flush with cake top. Repeat with other 3 dowel pieces, spacing evenly apart.

Place 8-inch cake tier on top of 10-inch cake, centering on bottom cake and resting the cake circle on the dowels in bottom cake. Brush top and sides of cake with apricot glaze. Brush fruit with remaining glaze. Arrange fresh fruit on sides of cake; pressing gently to secure

Center a piece of plastic wrap on top of the cake. Carefully place arrangement of fresh flowers on plastic wrap.

Italian Wedding Cake (recipe, page 91)

Recipe Index

APPETIZERS

Capellini Fritters 80
Mushroom Ravioli with
  Alfredo Sauce 28
Asiago Polenta with Mushroom Sauce 20
Baked Mostaccioli. 90
Baked Ravioli and Meatballs 16

BEEF

Baked Ravioli and Meatballs 16
Italian Sausage Sandwiches 34
Meatball Panini 33
Meatball Soup. 88
Rigatoni and Cheese Casserole
  with Pesto 58
Steak Italiano 42
Stuffed Cabbage Rolls. 26
Stuffed Peppers di Capri 54
Tuscan Pot Roast 68
Bow Ties with Artichoke Sauce 29
Brunch Frittata 62
Cake, Italian Wedding. 91
Capellini Fritters. 80

CASSEROLES

Baked Mostaccioli. 90
Baked Ravioli and Meatballs 16
Eggplant Parmigiana. 30
Lasagna Rolls with Eggplant and
  Prosciutto 23
Lasagna Roll-Ups Florentine 31
No-Boil Classic Lasagna 72
Rigatoni and Cheese Casserole
  with Pesto 58
Spinach and Cheese Stuffed Shells . . . 52
Stuffed Cabbage Rolls. 26
Stuffed Peppers di Capri 54

CHICKEN

Chicken Cacciatore 14
Chicken with Olives. 70
Garlic-Roasted Chicken Breasts 71
Lemon-and-Herb Roasted Chicken . . . 89
Pasta with Chicken and Sausage 41
Prosciutto- and Sage-Stuffed Chicken
  Rolls 78
Spicy Chicken and Penne Florentine . . 60
Venetian Chicken in Spicy
  Cream Sauce 59
Creamy Linguine with Smoked Salmon . . . 49
Eggplant Parmigiana. 30
Fettuccine with Shrimp and Mussels 76
Fire-Roasted Tomato and Garlic Pizza 13

FISH

Creamy Linguine with Smoked
  Salmon 49
Italian Fish Soup 25
Sea Bass with Tomato Pesto 40
Frittata, Brunch 62
Fritters, Capellini 80
Fusilli with Artichoke Hearts. 53
Garlic-Roasted Chicken Breasts 71
Gnocchi, Spinach 82
Grilled Sausages with Pepper-Onion
  Sauté. 87
Grilled Vegetable Pizza 12
Hearty Pasta di Toscana. 69
Italian Fish Soup 25
Italian Sausage Sandwiches 34
Italian Wedding Cake 91

LAMB

Lamb Chops and Cannellini 55
Pasta with Lamb Sauce 19
Lasagna Rolls with Eggplant
  and Prosciutto 23
Lasagna Roll-Ups Florentine 31
Lemon-and-Herb Roasted Chicken 89
Meatball Panini. 33
Meatball Soup 88

Recipe Index continued

MEATLESS MAIN DISHES

Brunch Frittata. 62
Eggplant Parmigiana. 30
Fusilli with Artichoke Hearts 53
Lasagna Roll-Ups Florentine 31
Roasted Vegetables and Pasta di
    Siena. 56
Spinach and Cheese Stuffed Shells . . . 52
Mushroom Ravioli with Alfredo Sauce 28
No-Boil Classic Lasagna 72
Pasta with Chicken and Sausage 41
Pasta with Lamb Sauce 19
Penne with Vodka. 24

PIZZAS

Fire-Roasted Tomato and Garlic
    Pizza. 13
Grilled Vegetable Pizza 12
Pizza Rustica 37
Polenta with Mushroom Sauce, Asiago. . . . 20

PORK

Penne with Vodka 24
Pork Medallions Arrabbiata. 47
Rigatoni with Ham and Peas 45
Stuffed Peppers di Capri 54

PROSCIUTTO

Lasagna Rolls with Eggplant and
    Prosciutto 23
Prosciutto- and Sage-Stuffed Chicken
    Rolls 78
Rigatoni with Ham and Peas 45
Rigatoni and Cheese Casserole with
    Pesto 58
Rigatoni with Ham and Peas 45
Risotto with Spinach and Herbs. 27
Roasted Potatoes. 90
Roasted Vegetables and Pasta di Siena . . . 56
Rotini Puttanesca 75

SANDWICHES

Italian Sausage Sandwiches. 34
Meatball Panini 33
Vegetable Calzones 32

SAUSAGE

Baked Mostaccioli. 90
Grilled Sausages with Pepper-Onion
    Sauté. 87
Italian Sausage Sandwiches 34
Meatball Panini 33
No-Boil Classic Lasagna 72
Pizza Rustica 37
Soup di Napoli. 50
Stuffed Cabbage Rolls. 26
Sea Bass with Tomato Pesto. 40

SEAFOOD

Fettuccine with Shrimp and Mussels. . 76
Italian Fish Soup 25
Shells with Spicy Seafood Sauce 44
Shrimp with Roasted Garlic Sauce. . . . 48
Shells with Spicy Seafood Sauce 44
Shrimp with Roasted Garlic Sauce 48

SIDE DISHES

Asiago Polenta with Mushroom
    Sauce 20
Bow Ties with Artichoke Sauce 29
Risotto with Spinach and Herbs 27
Roasted Potatoes 90
Rotini Puttanesca 75
Spinach Gnocchi 82
Vegetable and Bean Soup 64

SOUPS AND STEWS

Italian Fish Soup 25
Meatball Soup 88
Soup di Napoli. 50
Veal Stew 79
Vegetable and Bean Soup 64

Recipe Index *continued*

Spicy Chicken and Penne Florentine 60
Spinach and Cheese Stuffed Shells 52
Spinach Gnocchi 82
Steak Italiano 42
Stuffed Cabbage Rolls 26
Stuffed Peppers di Capri 54

TURKEY

Hearty Pasta di Toscana 69
Stuffed Cabbage Rolls 26
Tuscan Pot Roast 68

VEAL

Stuffed Peppers di Capri 54
Veal Cutlets with Tomato and Basil
Sauce 18
Veal Stew 79
Vegetable and Bean Soup 64
Vegetable Calzones 32
Venetian Chicken in Spicy Cream Sauce . . 59

TIPS

Antipasto Ideas 89
Assembling the Italian Wedding
Cake 92
Classic Flavors 27
Flavor with Pesto 40
Florentine Style, The 72
Fresh Herb Hints 49
From Bread to Bruschetta 79
Grilled Vegetables 12
Herbs of Italy, The 65
Little Dumplings 82
Mushrooms to Savor 14
Olive Branch, The 55
Pasta Sauce to the Rescue 69
Pasta Shapes and Sizes 22
Save the Jar 59
Say Pecorino Cheese 25
Serving Olive Oil 80
Serving Prosciutto 45
Shaped Pasta to Stuff 53
Shortcut Meatballs 33
Soup's On! 50
Sweet Note, A 19
Taste of Tuscany, A 71
Versatile Polenta 20
Wedding Feast, The 86
Wines of Italy, The 83